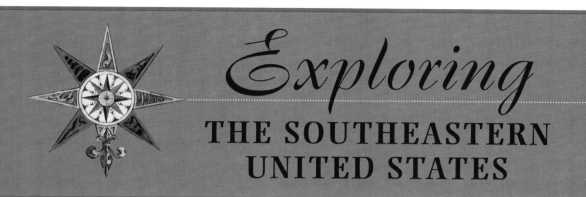

Exploring
THE SOUTHEASTERN UNITED STATES

Rose Blue and Corinne J. Naden

Raintree
Chicago, Illinois

For information, address the publisher:

Raintree
100 N. LaSalle
Suite 1200
Chicago IL 60602

07 06 05 04 03
10 9 8 7 6 5 4 3 2 1

Library of Congress Cataloging-in-Publication Data:

Blue, Rose.
  Exploring the southeastern United States / Rose
Blue and Corinne J.Naden.
     v. cm. -- (Exploring the Americas)
Includes bibliographical references (p.) and index.
Contents: Prologue: who found it? -- Juan Ponce de
Leon: Florida for the king (1513-21) -- Panfilo de
Narvaez: conquistador on an ill-fated mission
(1520-28) -- Hernando de Soto: to the Great River
(1538-42) -- Pedro Menendez de Aviles: founder of St.
Augustine (1565) -- Daniel Boone: explorer American
style (1775-78) -- Epilogue: what did they find? --
Important events in the exploration of southeastern
North America.
  ISBN 0-7398-4951-4 (HC), 1-4109-0045-2 (Pbk.)
  1. Southern States--Discovery and exploration--
Juvenile literature. 2. Explorers--Southern States--
Biography--Juvenile literature. [1. Southern States--
Discovery and exploration. 2. Explorers.] I. Naden,
Corinne J. II. Title. III. Series: Blue, Rose.
Exploring the Americas.
F212 . B57 2003
975'.01--dc21
                              2002013355

Acknowledgments
The author and publishers are grateful to the following for permission to reproduce copyright material:

Cover photographs by SuperStock, (map) Corbis

p. 4 Christie's Images/SuperStock; p. 6 Lee
Snider/Corbis; pp. 7, 12, 18, 20, 35, 46, 50, 58
Bettmann/Corbis; p. 9 Wolfgang Kaehler/Corbis;
p. 10 Tim Thompson/Corbis; p. 15 John
Farmar/Cordaiy Photo Library Ltd./Corbis; p. 16 Paul
A. Souders/Corbis; p. 21 Charles E. Rotkin/Corbis;
p. 23 Kevin Fleming/Corbis; p. 24 Vince
Streano/Corbis; pp. 26, 36, 41, 48 Hulton
Archive/Getty Images; pp. 28, 54 Archivo
Iconografico, S. A./Corbis; p. 30 Gordon Miller; p. 32
Alison Wright/Corbis; p. 34 Kennan Ward/Corbis;
p. 39 Lowell Georgia/Corbis; p. 40 Pierre
Perrin/Corbis SYGMA; p. 42 National Library of
Canada; p. 44 Kevin Schafer/Corbis; p. 47 Hubert
Stadler/Corbis

Photo research by Alyx Kellington

Every effort has been made to contact copyright
holders of any material reproduced in this book.
Any omissions will be rectified in subsequent printings
if notice is given to the publisher.

Some words are shown in bold, like **this.** You can find
out what they mean by looking in the Glossary.

Contents

Prologue:
Who Found It?

What were they looking for? And why? The early explorers sailed from Europe for many reasons. They all were eager to seek out the unknown. Some people are thrilled by new things. They live for the pure adventure of exploring a huge dark cave or dropping hundreds of feet to the murky bottom of the sea. Sailing across the Atlantic in the 1500s would certainly have been adventurous.

Although most people no longer thought that the earth was flat, they did believe two things about the world that were totally wrong. They thought that the earth was mostly land, about a ratio of seven parts land to one part water. Today, we know that the earth is nearly all water, more than 70 percent. Also, most people, including the early explorers, believed the earth to be about 20 percent smaller than it really is. The distance around the equator is 24,902 miles (40,076 kilometers). Early calculations put it at 20,400 miles (32,831 kilometers). Perhaps it was just as well that Christopher Columbus, on his first voyage, did not know how large the earth was. Since he thought he was going to Asia, how could he have signed up a crew for what really was a journey of about 12,000 miles (1,931 kilometers)?

Besides adventure, some explorers were looking for a northwest passage to the Far East. Most sought new lands to

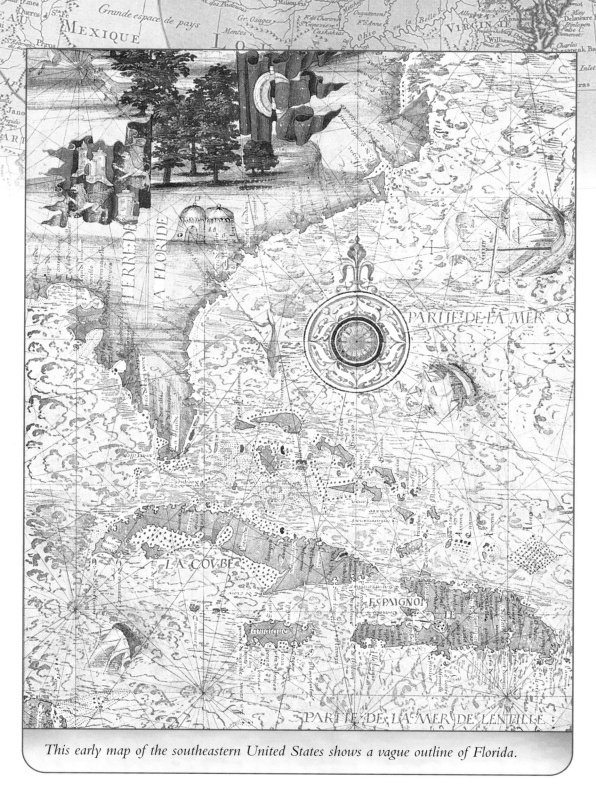

This early map of the southeastern United States shows a vague outline of Florida.

claim for European kings and queens. And, to one degree or another, all of them were interested in gold. Four of the five explorers included in this book sailed for Spain. They were definitely looking for gold and other precious metals. That was what Spain wanted when it began exploring what Europeans were calling the New World. Spanish adventurers wanted quick wealth to bring back home. They also sailed for the glory of Spain. When Spain conquered new lands, it set up huge plantations that were worked by tenants or native peoples. As a result, Spanish colonies did not attract the European middle or working classes the way that English or French colonies did.

Sixteenth-century explorers from Spain are called "conquistadors." It means conqueror. In general, they earned a well-deserved bad reputation. Their treatment of native peoples was often brutal and cruel. Yet, Spain, unlike other European countries, sent missionaries with the explorers. At the same time many of the explorers were terrorizing native peoples, monks were trying to convert them to Christianity.

This book covers four Spaniards and one American who left their impressions on what became the southeastern United States. Juan Ponce de Leon sailed on the second voyage of Christopher Columbus, later becoming the first European to see

and name Puerto Rico and Florida. Soldier and adventurer Panfilo de Narvaez was sent on a mission to colonize the territory of Florida. He was brave but cruel and not a very good choice for the job. Hernando de Soto is given credit as the first European to see the Mississippi River and the first to explore southeastern North America. Pedro Menendez de Aviles founded St. Augustine, Florida, the first permanent white settlement in what became the United States.

The fifth explorer in this group lived long after the others. And he is not usually thought of as an explorer. He was Daniel Boone, an American-born frontiersman with the familiar **coonskin** cap. But he did explore the southeastern United States. His trailblazing through the Appalachians helped to open the American West and settle what became the state of Kentucky.

This exploration of the southeastern United States begins in the late 1400s. Little was known about the huge land that Columbus had first encountered in 1492. But by the time Daniel Boone was trekking through the wilderness, the Spanish were well-settled in the southeast. The French were active around the Gulf of Mexico, and the English had a firm colonial hold in the north.

Explorers, especially the early ones, are said to have "discovered" things— new lands, a mountain, a river. But

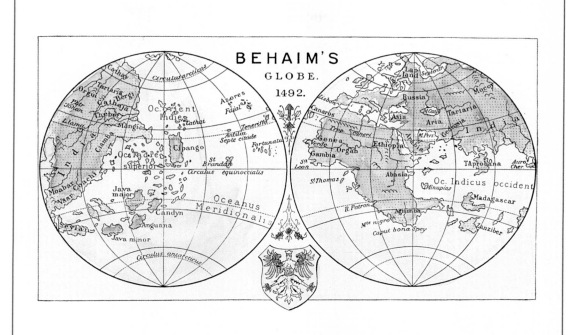

This early map shows how Europeans viewed the world at the time of Columbus.

generally speaking, these men were not the first to find the land, the mountain, or the river. And in most cases, when the explorers "found" a place, someone was already living there.

European explorers were not usually the first to find anything. But they are important in our history because they recorded what they saw. They wrote in their journals about their voyages. They made maps that Europe had never seen before. In fact, most of Europe had never even known that two continents existed beyond the Atlantic Ocean. A new world came to life for the people of Europe. As more and more adventurers followed the early explorers, they began to change the known world. And that is why they still fascinate us today.

Chapter One
Juan Ponce De Leon
Florida for the King (1513–1521)

If Christopher Columbus is the European discoverer of the Americas, then Juan Ponce de Leon (c.1460–1521) must be called the European discoverer of North America. While he was looking for the fountain of eternal youth, Ponce de Leon came upon Florida. The fabled fountain of youth is just one of many legends that have hung on through the years, like the Loch Ness monster in Scotland or the sunken continent of Atlantis. Some people still think that the Loch Ness monster exists; others say that Atlantis really did sink. Perhaps some are still looking for the fountain of youth; if so, no one has found it. Still, it seemed like a real possibility in the 1500s.

Ponce de Leon heard Native American tales of a wondrous spring on an island called Bimini. Whoever drank from it or bathed in it would be restored to youth. So, in 1513 the Spanish conquistador went in search of these miraculous waters in the swamps of what is now Florida. It is said that every legend, no matter how silly it may seem to modern ears, has at least some logic to it. The springs in the swampy area of Florida are generally quite cool. This contrast with the usually hot summer air makes for a very refreshing experience. The springs do not, as far as we know, restore anyone's youth, but they probably do make the bather jump around for a while!

Ponce de Leon never found the fountain of youth. But in his search, he trekked from east to west and claimed what he thought was an island for his king. He named it Florida. Six years later, Ponce de Leon died in Puerto Rico, where he founded that island's oldest settlement.

A portrait of Juan Ponce de Leon (1460–1521)

The map shows:

Gulf of Mexico
St. John's River (Daytona)
Cape Canaveral
Tampa Bay (Sarasota)
Peace River
Lake Okeechobee
Atlantic Ocean
Charlotte Harbor
Caloosahatchee River
(Miami)
Dry Tortugas
(Key West)
Florida Keys
HAVANA
THE BAHAMAS
N
CUBA
1513
1521
BELIZE
JAMAICA
HAITI
DOM. REP.
PUERTO RICO

225 km
0
200 Miles

— Route 1513
— Route 1521

Ponce de Leon's travels took him around the the southern part of the Florida panhandle.

The time of the conquistadors

Juan Ponce de Leon was a conquistador. The name refers to Spanish explorers sent out to conquer America in the sixteenth century. They were men such as Hernan Cortes, Hernando de Soto, Francisco Pizarro, and Ponce de Leon. By and large, these men were not interested in settling or governing a region. They were interested in finding gold and fighting for it. When Spain decided that it was time to settle down in the Americas, the conquistadors were quickly replaced by those who knew how to administer and settle a colony.

Conquistadors in general have a bad reputation. There are enough examples of their brutality in handling native peoples to believe that they earned this reputation. Ponce de Leon was a man of his time, probably no more or less harsh than the next. He would have understood little of today's concerns about human rights. Victory for Spain was always more important to him than anything else.

This raised portrait depicts Ferdinand and Isabella, the king and queen of Spain.

Of noble birth

Ponce de Leon was born into a noble family probably around 1460 and likely in Tierra de Campos, Palencia, Spain. Both sides of his family, the Ponces and the Leons, had held great wealth and prestige in the region of Aragon. However, the wealth and prestige had vanished by the mid-1400s. That left the young man without the money to pursue a military career.

So he did the next best thing for him. He appealed to a wealthy nobleman, Don Pedro Nunez de Guzman. Don Pedro, honoring the reputation of the young man's family, allowed him to become a page in the royal court of Aragon. Don Pedro also allowed him to spend his spare hours with a teacher who trained him in military matters. The teacher was impressed enough with his diligence and hard work to recommend the young man as a knight-in-training. Thus, Ponce de Leon became a soldier in Don Pedro's private army, eventually becoming the don's personal **squire.**

When war erupted, Don Pedro's army went into battle. In 1476, the Battle of Toro was fought between the armies of the Spanish monarchs, Ferdinand and Isabella, and Alfonso V of Portugal. Spain won, and Ponce de Leon so distinguished himself in the fight that he was knighted on the battlefield. Promoted to captain in Don Pedro's army, he also fought against the Moors in Spain for nearly a decade. Spain had been in turmoil for centuries, but it had united under the Catholic king and queen. They wanted to drive the Moors, who were Muslims, out of the country.

Spain won that fight, too, but now the land was in ruins. There was little hope of a prosperous future for many of the young nobleman, called hidalgos, who had backed the crown. These included Ponce de Leon.

To the New World

In the spring of 1493, some astonishing news began to spread throughout Europe. It completely changed the life and career of Juan Ponce de Leon. Several months earlier, on August 3, 1492, Christopher Columbus, an Italian explorer in the service of Spain, had sailed west to find a passage to the Far East. He returned with a story that seemed more unbelievable than the legends of centuries past. Although Columbus at first believed that he had reached the Indies—hence, the term "Indians"—he had in fact encountered what was for Europe a strange new world. Indeed, "New World" is what the Europeans began to call this unknown land far across the Atlantic.

On that voyage, Columbus had reached an island in the Bahamas that he claimed for Spain, naming it San Salvador. From there, he sailed to what is now Haiti. Columbus thought it so beautiful that he named it Espanola (Hispaniola), the "Spanish island." Today, Hispaniola refers to the second largest island in the West Indies, divided into Haiti and the Dominican Republic.

When Isabella and Ferdinand heard the news, they could hardly wait to send Columbus on a second voyage before their archenemy Portugal got there. Indeed, the royal monarchs had some reason to worry. When Columbus had returned from the first voyage in 1493, he landed on the Portuguese coast and was invited to see the king. John II said that any lands Columbus discovered belonged to Portugal by virtue of the Treaty of Alcacovas, which Spain and Portugal had signed in 1479. The treaty was supposed to mark clearly any future claims on newly discovered lands by the two countries. However, both sides

Columbus arrives in the New World.

seem to have interpreted it differently, and Isabella and Ferdinand at once appealed to Pope Alexander VI.

The pope, himself a Spaniard, solved the problem for Spain. He issued four Bulls, or declarations, giving the newly discovered lands to Spain. In 1494, Spain and Portugal signed the Treaty of Tordesillas, which drew a north-south line west of the Cape Verde Islands. Everything west of the line was to go to Spain, everything east to Portugal. The treaty remained in effect until 1750.

Satisfied that his discoveries would go to Spain, Columbus planned his second voyage. It was more ambitious than the first. Instead of three ships, this was a **flotilla** of 17 vessels and about 1,500 people. In addition to seeking gold and claiming land, the Spaniards intended to convert the native peoples they encountered to Christianity and teach them how to cultivate the soil.

It was Don Pedro who suggested that Ponce de Leon go along with Columbus on his second voyage. Bored with chasing after the Moors, the young man agreed. He joined a long list of those volunteering for the expedition to the Americas. This would be his reward for service to the crown. He was accepted and put in charge of 60 soldiers.

The second voyage of Columbus sailed with the morning tide from Cadiz, Spain, on September 25, 1493. After crossing the Atlantic, Columbus stopped briefly in the Bahamas and then at the island of Puerto Rico to look for freshwater. Ponce de Leon was apparently among the first Europeans to set foot on what he later called Porto (Puerto) Rico, which means "rich port."

But Columbus was in a hurry to get to Hispaniola. He had left 40 of his men at Haiti on his first voyage. What he found now was disaster. Columbus had told his men to build a village, plant crops, and form a permanent settlement, called La Villa de la Navidad, or Nativity Town. But the Spaniards were more anxious to look for gold, so they pressed the native peoples into service as slaves while they searched for a fortune that was not there. Eventually, the Native Americans grew tired of this treatment and killed most of the Spaniards.

This was the beginning of what became a difficult relationship between Spain and Native American peoples. On his first voyage, Columbus had found them to be friendly and helpful. But now the native peoples understood what could happen to them. As for the Spanish, they seemed to have learned little from this incident, because it was repeated time and again in the Americas.

The subject of slavery

Ponce de Leon returned to Spain with Columbus in 1496 but was back in the West Indies in 1502. This time he left behind a wife, Inez, a son, and a daughter. His new job was to serve under Nicolas de Ovando, appointed governor of Hispaniola. But there was continuing trouble in the islands. Queen Isabella ordered the native peoples to become Christians. However, most of the Spaniards in the New World were more interested in working the Native Americans to death in the search for gold. Isabella died in 1504, and King Ferdinand was inclined to look the other way in matters concerning slavery. He regarded it as just another way to make money for Spain.

Soon after he reached Hispaniola, Ponce de Leon was sent on a two-year fight against the Higuey people on the eastern part of the island, in what is now the Dominican Republic. The trouble started when a Spaniard's dog killed a Native American. Ponce de Leon subdued the Higuey in 1504. As a reward, he was named *adelantado* (provincial governor) for eastern Hispaniola.

This was a centuries-old system in Spain. At first the *adelantado* had been merely a licensed agent of the monarch. But after the long fight with the Moors, richer estates were awarded for loyal service. The governor had the right to demand payment or forced labor from generally peaceful native peoples. The Native Americans were supposed to be fed, housed, and protected in return. That did not always occur, however. They were also supposed to be instructed in the Catholic faith. This system was not regarded as slavery by the Spaniards, but it did, however, treat Native Americans as children who could not care for themselves.

Why were most European explorers so ready to look upon Native Americans

This house was built by Ponce de Leon in Hispaniola.

as inferior to themselves and, therefore, easy to enslave? A part of this acceptance stemmed from the writings of the great Greek philosopher Aristotle (384–322 B.C.E.). In his **doctrine** of natural slavery, Aristotle claimed that some people are naturally inferior and, therefore, can be properly enslaved. Even those who did not agree tended to view certain people, such as the poor and uneducated of European society, as those who are born to serve others. Almost without exception, the explorers considered Native Americans to be grossly inferior to themselves, as well as savage and ignorant. From that viewpoint, slavery was an easy step for them.

Off to Puerto Rico

As governor of Hispaniola, Ponce de Leon received a few hundred acres of land on which he raised cattle and vegetables. Because every Spanish ship returning to the home country stopped at Hispaniola for provisions, Ponce de Leon did not have to search for gold. Supplying the ships with farm goods made him very wealthy.

Ponce de Leon's family joined him on Hispaniola. But before long, the explorer was gone again. It was hard to resist the lure of gold. Hearing tales of great wealth on an island that the native peoples called Borinquen, Ponce de Leon got permission from Ovando to sail there in 1507 or 1508.

For about a year, he explored the island that he named Puerto Rico. He founded its oldest settlement, Caparra, near the present-day capital of San Juan. Having generally subdued the native peoples, he returned to Hispaniola. For his work, Ovando recommended that the conquistador be appointed *adelantado* of the island.

With his family, Ponce de Leon settled down to govern Puerto Rico. It proved a difficult task. Not surprisingly, many of the native people resented the loss of their freedom and did not take kindly to Spanish rule. Ponce de Leon spent much of his time hunting the runaways. Some reports say he imported greyhound dogs, which the Spanish used on Hispaniola to track the Native Americans who fled. The dogs' ability to track and sniff out fugitives terrorized the native peoples.

Ponce de Leon might have stayed on for years as governor of Puerto Rico. He was apparently happy there and was becoming a rich man. But in 1512 politics got in the way. He was frequently at odds with the other Spaniards appointed to key posts on the island. So the aging conquistador began to have thoughts about another job.

For some time, he had heard Native American tales about a miraculous spring on an island called Bimini, north of Hispaniola. It was said that a drink from its waters could restore youth and vigor to anyone. Such tales would not have been new to Ponce de Leon. He had probably heard a similar story as a boy. And it was not too fantastic to think that a fountain of youth might exist in this strange new world. So, Ponce de Leon decided to go in search of it.

Finding Florida

He applied for a royal patent on February 23, 1512. Rather than saying he was looking for a magic fountain, he said he wanted to explore new land, find gold, and produce new slaves. All that was true as well. Permission was granted, and nothing was said in the contract about looking for a fountain of youth. However, the term remains forever linked with the explorations of Ponce de Leon.

A painting romanticizes Ponce de Leon's quest for the legendary fountain of youth.

taking the new land for Spain. Most records say he landed near present-day St. Augus-tine, but some scholars think the landing was actually to the south, near what is now Daytona Beach. Wherever he was, Ponce de Leon thought he had found the island of the miraculous spring. He named it Florida, for the Easter festival of Pascua Florida that had occurred a few days earlier. Thus he is credited with being the first European to step upon what became the 38th state of the United States of America. Many explorers who followed him would also believe that Florida was an island. That mistake would not be corrected until six years later when another Spaniard, Alonso Alvarez de Pineda, arrived. He was the first European to map the coast of Florida, and he did so fairly accurately.

Around April 8, the three ships pulled anchor and sailed northward for a short time, then turned south and hugged the coastline. On occasion, they saw Native Americans on the shore, the first they had encountered on the trip.

After about two weeks, the flotilla ran into a very strong current. It was so strong that the *San Cristobal* just drifted out to sea. It was two days before the ship was able to return. Ponce de Leon

As was the general rule, the patent gave him the title of *adelantado* as well as authority over this new land for his lifetime. However, outfitting the expedition was his problem. That, too, was the custom. For the crown, this was a win-win situation.

Ponce de Leon, then about 39 years old, left Puerto Rico on March 4, 1513. With him sailed a small **flotilla** of three ships, the *Santiago, Santa Maria de Consolacion*, and the *San Cristobal*. The chief pilot was Anton de Alaminos, of Palos, Spain. They sailed northward to the Bahama Islands, then westward.

On April 2, the small flotilla spotted land. What Ponce de Leon saw was a long smudge of uncharted Florida coast, which he thought was a large island. He quickly rowed ashore and planted a flag, did not know it, of course, but he had just sailed into the Gulf Stream. He was the first to describe its effects.

On the sail south along the Florida coast, the small expedition occasionally encountered groups of native peoples. Some were friendly, some were not. In one skirmish, the explorers captured a Native American who served as their guide and interpreter. After they rounded the Florida cape, they sailed past what is now Key West and onto a series of small rocky islands now called the Marquesas Keys. There, Calusa people traded with them. They spoke of a chief who had gold to sell. So, Ponce de Leon sailed up the western coast of Florida, still believ-

The Marquesas Keys are a series of ten islands, surrounded by shallow water and reef.

ing it was an island. He anchored in Charlotte Harbor, south of present-day Sarasota. But instead of trading for gold, the Native Americans attacked, although little harm was done to either side.

After that encounter, however, it seemed like a smart idea to turn around. Sailing south again, this time the **flotilla** found the islands called the Dry Tortugas. There was no gold there, but Ponce de Leon and his men were amazed by what they did see. It was wildlife such as the Spaniards never knew existed. The Dry Tortugas were filled with giant sea turtles, seals, gentle manatees, and countless birds and other wildlife. The men killed many of the giant turtles to take with them.

Ponce de Leon then directed the expedition back toward Puerto Rico. Once they reached the Bahamas, the *San Cristobal* went down, although the crew was saved. Leaving the *Santa Maria* to continue the search for the wondrous fountain, Ponce de Leon returned to Puerto Rico in the *Santiago*. He had been sailing for seven months. He had found little or no gold and certainly no magic spring that would bring back youth. But he had claimed, not an island as he thought, but a huge parcel of land for his king.

Ponce de Leon was well aware of his achievement, even though he did not know the extent of it. Now, he wanted to make sure that King Ferdinand knew about it, too.

Plans to colonize

In 1514 Ponce de Leon returned to Spain and had an audience with the king. Well pleased with the new lands in his name, King Ferdinand gave the conquistador a grant to colonize both Puerto Rico and Florida. Ponce de Leon was named military governor of both regions.

The new governor was back in Puerto Rico in 1515, but it would be several years before he saw Florida again. For one thing, he had to return to Spain the next year. King Ferdinand had died and the throne was now occupied by his grandson, Carlos I, who later became Charles V, emperor of the Holy Roman Empire. Although Ponce de Leon's loyalty to the crown was unquestioned, he wanted to make sure that his privileges were secure under a new ruler. He remained in Spain until the spring of 1518.

Florida on his mind

When Ponce de Leon returned to Puerto Rico, he noted a few changes. For one, his soon to be son-in-law, Antonio de la Gama, was about to become governor of the island. For another, the people of Caparra, the settlement Ponce de Leon had founded, moved to an island in the harbor. It was called El Puerto Rico de San Juan, or the rich port of San Juan. Today it is Old San Juan. It is the oldest city that flies the American flag, now that Puerto Rico is part of the United States.

But Ponce de Leon had Florida on his mind and planned to found a settlement there. So, he set sail from San Juan on February 20, 1521, with about 200 men and two ships loaded with seeds, 50 horses, and other livestock. Very little is known about this second voyage except that it did not succeed.

The small expedition probably landed once again at Charlotte Harbor on Florida's western coast. Over the next few months, the group searched for the best site to start a colony. But in early July 1521, a fierce fight took place between Ponce de Leon's crew and a band of Native Americans.

The Spaniards were outnumbered and not many survived. Ponce de Leon was wounded in the thigh by a poisoned arrow. In a panic, the next in command ordered all survivors to return to the ships. In haste, they sailed for Cuba.

Ponce de Leon died of his wound in Havana. In 1559, his remains were moved to the San Juan Cathedral. Puerto Rico's third largest city, Ponce, is named for him.

Juan Ponce de Leon was not an outstanding personality in the often larger-than-life portraits of early explorers. He was loyal to his country and carried out his orders with hard work and determination. In so doing, he helped to open southeastern North America—especially Florida—for all the settlers to come.

Chapter Two

Panfilo de Narvaez
Conquistador on an Ill-Fated Mission (1520–1528)

Conquistador Panfilo de Narvaez (1478–1528) does not fare well in the history books. He was apparently brave but also cruel and not very competent. In fact, in *The European Discovery of America*, author Samuel Eliot Morison calls Narvaez "the most incompetent of all who sailed for Spain in this era." That was most unfortunate because his ineptness apparently caused the failure of his expedition and cost him his own life as well as the lives of his men. After gaining fame during the conquest of Cuba, he was sent on a mission to explore Mexico and Florida. Then as now, what seems like a good plan does not always end well.

A military life

Born in Valladolid, Spain in about 1478, Narvaez, like so many young men of his time, sought a career in the military as a way to fame and fortune. Apparently he had already gained a modest reputation as a soldier when he emigrated to the island of Hispaniola, now shared by Haiti and the Dominican Republic, in 1498. In 1509, he went to Jamaica with Juan de Esquival to take it for the Spanish crown.

Christopher Columbus had reached Jamaica in 1494 and was later shipwrecked there for a year. Esquival

A statue depicts Panfilo de Narvaez (1478–1528)

founded the first settlement at Sevilla la Nueva (now an archaeological site) on the north coast. But Spanish settlement was particularly disastrous to the native peoples there. They quickly died from diseases brought by the Europeans. By the beginning of the 1600s, virtually none of the native Arawak population was left on the island of Jamaica.

Terror in Cuba

Next, Spain turned its attention to Cuba. Columbus had stopped there during his first voyage in 1492. Now, in 1511, Diego Velazquez was ordered to the island, along with specially trained archers, to take control as the governor. Since Velazquez was an old friend, Narvaez requested and received permission to accompany him.

The conquest of Cuba by the Spaniards was ruthless and brutal. In five years, the island had been divided into seven separate divisions. Within 40 years, the native population would be decimated, due largely to disease and maltreatment. During the conquest of Cuba, Narvaez gained his reputation for outstanding bravery, as well as for excessive cruelty. Father Bartolome de las Casas, a priest who went on the expedition and was a champion of human rights, later wrote that the taking of Cuba was a bloody slaughter. He cited Narvaez as having personally killed some 2,000 Native Americans.

For his service in Cuba, Narvaez was rewarded. He became special agent and accountant for the island and was granted large parcels of land. He also married a wealthy widow, Maria de Valenzuela, who was herself a huge landowner. In his civilian position, Narvaez actually tried to do some good things for Cuba, such as petitioning the crown for money to build roads.

Father Bartolome de las Casas spoke out against Narvaez's cruelty to native peoples.

The first disaster

In 1520, Governor Velazquez selected Narvaez for an important job. The year before, explorer Hernan Cortes had landed in what is now Veracruz, Mexico, and established the first Spanish settlement. Then, Cortes had proceeded inland to conquer the territory for himself. This irritated Spain and infuriated Velazquez, who ordered Narvaez to go to Mexico to kill or capture Cortes, who was charged with treason.

A rather impressive fleet, the largest ever assembled in the Americas, was assigned to the task. Narvaez commanded 18 ships, 900 crew, and about 1,000 Native Americans. Named captain-general of the Mexican Conquest, a higher ranking than that of Cortes, Narvaez sailed for Mexico and landed at Veracruz on April 23, 1520.

There was little doubt that Panfilo de Narvaez was militarily qualified for the task. And he was surely brave enough, perhaps too brave. His bravado made him arrogant. He was not inclined to listen to anyone else's advice. While Narvaez set up camp and sent messengers to talk to Cortes, the clever Cortes was busy engineering a surprise attack. The two forces clashed at Cempoala, on the road to Mexico City, on May 23. Considering the fact that Cortes was outnumbered five to one, the battle was amazingly short. Narvaez not only lost the fight, but lost one eye as well. His ships were dismantled, and Narvaez and his men were taken prisoner. The men were soon recruited into Cortes's army, although Narvaez was left in jail for a year. In the meantime, Cortes went on with the task of conquering Mexico.

An illustration shows Santo Domingo in the time of Narvaez.

Narvaez did do great damage to Mexico, however. One of his crew members carried the deadly smallpox virus. During the **epidemic** that followed in 1520–1521, thousands of Native Mexicans died.

Voyage to Florida

In August 1521, Narvaez was released on orders from the crown and returned to Cuba. But undefeated even in defeat, he went to Spain to seek permission from Charles V to conquer and settle Florida. His friends thought he was crazy, but the king obviously did not. Narvaez was given various titles and grants with the right to subdue and settle lands in Florida westward.

Narvaez sailed from San Lucar, Spain, on the morning tide of June 17, 1527. With him went five ships and 600 soldiers, sailors, colonists, and priests, including Alvar Nunez Cabeza de Vaca as treasurer. He would be one of four survivors of the ill-fated voyage.

Narvaez landed at Santo Domingo and remained for 45 days. That was long enough for 140 men to desert the expedition. Enough men were pressed into service from the native population to make up the loss, and a sixth ship was added.

The next stop was Cuba, which the fleet reached in early September. Their problem this time was a hurricane off the Cuban coast. It caused the loss of two ships, 50 men, and 20 horses. Narvaez decided to spend the winter on the island at Trinidad.

On February 20, 1528, Narvaez got the expedition going again. It was now down to 400 men and 80 horses. He had purchased another ship so now there were five, and he planned to sail to Havana to pick up one more, along with additional soldiers. Unfortunately for Narvaez, he never got to Havana. This time the fault was apparently due to his incompetent navigator and pilot, Diego Miruelo. He managed to run the whole fleet aground off Cuba's southern coast, and they were stuck for fifteen days.

Although the ships got free at last, bad luck continued to follow the mis-

A painting of Charles V

sion. Severe storms prevented the vessels from entering the Havana harbor. Instead, they were blown northward all the way to near Tampa Bay or Charlotte Harbor on Florida's west coast. They anchored on April 14, 1528.

The following day, Narvaez and some of his men went ashore. On April 16, he performed the ritual of taking the land for the Spanish crown. Requirements were recited for the benefit of the native peoples, even though no Native Americans were there. Narvaez warned that if the native population did not obey the pope, the head of the Catholic Church, and the Spanish king, men, women, and children would be subject to slavery or death. It mattered little whether Native Americans, even if they had been present at the ceremony, would have understood what was said or have had knowledge of the pope or the Spanish crown.

If the Native Americans did not obey, Narvaez continued, their slavery or death would be their own fault, not the crown's and certainly not his. These warnings were standard operating procedures for the conquistadors as they claimed land in the Americas.

The wrong decision

After searching the area for several weeks and finding nothing more than some hostile Native Americans, Narvaez made a terrible decision. It would eventually cost him his own life and the lives of most of his crew. Against the strong advice of Cabeza de Vaca, he decided to split his forces.

Narvaez kept 300 men and the remaining 40 horses with him for a march inland to the north. He had heard tales of great riches in a town called Apalache. He sent the rest of the men, about 100, and the ships to search the coast. They were under command of pilot Miruelo, who had earlier run them aground. But Miruelo, who had visited Florida on an earlier voyage, claimed to remember a safe harbor to the north. At this harbor, whose location no one knew, the two groups planned to reunite.

On the inland journey, Narvaez and his men ran into swamps, poisonous snakes, and alligators. The native peoples they met were hostile. However, when they captured a small group, Narvaez heard again of great deposits of gold in Apalache. He pushed on.

By mid-June, the expedition crossed the Suwanee River, where the first Spaniard was lost, then headed west along the Florida **panhandle.** For the next month, the party suffered greatly. The food supply was dwindling. They ate palm leaves and sometimes stole corn from local villages.

The native peoples in the area were generally hostile, which was largely the

A swamp in inland Florida

fault of the Spanish themselves. At one point they met a Native American chief who invited them to his home village, but the Europeans acted with such obnoxious behavior that the chief took back his offer of aid.

Finally, sometime in late June, the expedition found the town of Apalache, not far from Tallahassee, the present capital of Florida. The only gold they found was yellow corn growing in a village of about 40 huts. Angrily, they seized women and children as hostages. This brought a rain of arrows down upon the small expedition, which found itself nearly imprisoned in the village for nearly a month.

Narvaez decided that the only way out was to escape to the sea. They headed south toward the gulf. Thrashing through swamp and forests, constantly pursued by the hostile native peoples, the weary expedition reached present-day St. Marks in early September. The rescue ships were nowhere in sight.

Nor would they ever be. For nearly a year, Miruelo and the ships hunted for the safe harbor along the Florida coast. When it was not to be found, the seafarers gave up and sailed away for the safety of Veracruz in Mexico.

Journey home

Unknown to Narvaez at the time, he and his expedition were stranded. But there was no sign of the ships and hostile Native Americans blocked their way inland. So, Narvaez decided that they

Okefenokee Swamp covers an area of about 600 square miles (1,554 square kilometers) in northern Florida and southeastern Georgia.

must build their own small boats and sail down the Florida coast to Mexico. This was, indeed, a bold plan, except that Narvaez had not thought to include boatbuilders in the expedition and there was only one carpenter. There were no tools, no sails, and no nails. No one in the crew had the slightest idea of how to build a boat. Even worse, there was practically no food. The horses, one by one, had to be eaten. Occasionally, the men were able to raid a nearby Native American village for corn. Each day someone in the crew became too ill or too weak to work. Many died.

Yet, the Spanish were stubborn and inventive. They made nails and workable tools from anything iron that they carried with them. They made sails from their clothing. Rope came from the tails of the dead horses. Narvaez named the inlet where they worked the Bay of Horses in honor of the sacrificed animals.

The boat building took weeks. By late September, about 245 survivors crowded into five small, crudely built, and sometimes leaky vessels. Since no one in the party knew how to navigate, they decided to hug the coast as they sailed westward. Besides, they had to stop periodically to hunt for food. Several of the crew were killed while trying to steal food from Native American villages. The biggest problem, however, was lack of fresh water. The thirst was agonizing. Several men died from drinking salt water.

Near the end of October 1528, the half-dead expedition had drifted along the Gulf of Mexico and miraculously arrived at the mouth of the Mississippi River. But bad luck was not about to let go. Now a strong river current entered the gulf and broke the towlines that held the five boats. According to the later journal of Cabeza de Vaca, he called for a rope from Narvaez's craft, but the leader apparently replied that everyone had to save his own life.

Three of the small boats were blown out to sea, including that of Panfilo de Narvaez. He was never seen again.

The aftermath

Two of the boats drifted to what is now Galveston Island, Texas. Fifteen men, including Cabeza de Vaca, survived. His survival is perhaps the most dramatic story of the entire Narvaez expedition. Cabeza de Vaca was captured numerous times by native peoples, but managed to escape, sometimes by becoming a sort of medicine man for the Native Americans. In September 1534, along with Alonso del Castillo Maldonado, Andres Dorantes, and Esteban, a black Moroccan, he escaped his captors and began to wander around the Gulf region in present-day Texas. Finally, after crossing the Rio Grande into Mexico in April 1536, the thin, barely recognizable

Galveston Island is 51 miles (82 kilometers) southeast of Houston, Texas.

A painting depicts Alvar Nunez Cabeza de Vaca during his years of wandering in the Texas wilderness.

band was rescued. Nearly eight years after the fatal Narvaez expedition had set sail, they reached Mexico City in July.

Cabeza de Vaca returned to Spain, where he was welcomed at the royal court in 1537. His journal was published in 1542. He recorded fair and accurate descriptions of Native Americans. In fact, unlike many of the Spanish adventurers, he came to see Native Americans not as inferior beings but as equals who followed a different lifestyle and culture. He envisioned that two such different cultures could live together and under-

stand each other. Cabeza de Vaca also came to believe that cooperation was possible between the peoples of Spain and the Americas, a concept not readily accepted by most Spanish people.

The journal also contained vivid descriptions of the horrors of the journey. But, strangely enough, instead of deterring further exploration, they seemed to inspire great excitement in Spain. The North American continent, however forbidding, did not seem quite so mysterious. However barren some of the land might be, his descriptions presented a more accurate appreciation of its size.

Unlike Narvaez the conquistador, Cabeza de Vaca returned to lead a trail of new expeditions westward. He would later explore in South America also and is credited with being the first European to see the spectacular Iguaçu Falls. Located on the Argentina-Brazil border, it is four times the width of Niagara Falls in North America.

As for the one-eyed, red-bearded giant Panfilo de Narvaez, his story is more one of guts than of thoughtful leadership. Some say it was his temper that was responsible for his acts of brutality. For years after his death, other explorers in Florida found traces of his expedition, of the hardships and eventual fate of Narvaez and his men. His story is a reminder that not all of the early explorers in the Americas were successful in their missions.

Chapter Three

Hernando de Soto

Westward to the Mississippi (1538–1542)

Hernando de Soto (c.1500–1542) is high on the list of the world's great explorers. He was the first European to see the Mississippi River and the first to explore what would become the southeastern United States. He was one of Spain's most famous conquistadors. He was also one of its most infamous; his cruelty to native peoples was well known. He took part in the conquests of Central America and Peru.

A life of adventure

When Soto was born, in about 1500, Spain had only recently become a united nation. Centuries of war, fighting in the Crusades or with the Moors or with each other, had kept the land in constant turmoil. Not surprisingly, many Spanish boys dreamed of glory on the battlefield. Hernando was one of them.

He was born in the mountainous Extremadura province (now Badajoz) near the border of Portugal in a town called Jerez de los Caballeros. His family was of minor nobility but without money, and the boy spent his early years in the manor home. What little money the family had would go to Soto's older brother, so his mother hoped that perhaps Hernando would become a priest or a scholar. But he already had other ideas. His would be a life of adventure and glory for Spain and for himself.

By the time he was in his early teens, Soto was taller and stronger than most grown men. His father sent him to the city of Seville with a letter of introduction to Pedro Arias Davila, a wealthy nobleman, aging warrior, and strict disciplinarian. Known as Don Pedrarias, he was King Ferdinand's trusted military leader. Now, Pedrarias became the boy's patron. Some reports say the patron paid for Soto's education at the University of Salamanca.

A portrait of Hernando de Soto (c.1500–1542)

To Panama

In the year 1514, when Soto was probably only about 14 years old, he sailed to the Americas with Pedrarias, who had been appointed governor of Darien on the **isthmus** of Panama. A year earlier, explorer Vasco Nunez de Balboa was the first European to cross the isthmus and see the Pacific Ocean. Pedrarias would later have Balboa executed for treason. There had long been friction between the men. Pedrarias accused Balboa of rebellion and mistreatment of natives peoples, among other charges.

Soto, who was given the rank of captain, soon earned a reputation for bravery, boldness, and skill as a horseman. He also became quite wealthy by being well rewarded with gold and slaves. In addition, he proved to be a clever businessman, forming a partnership with two other conquistadors to divide any plundered loot equally.

In 1523, Pedrarias sent his young officer to Nicaragua, acting as lieutenant to Hernandez de Cordoba. The mission was to unseat a Pedrarias rival. However, once in Nicaragua, Cordoba decided to take over the region himself. Soto refused to betray Pedrarias and was imprisoned, but he escaped and reported back to his patron. Pedrarias was so angry that he marched to Nicaragua himself, overthrew Cordoba,

and killed him. Soto settled in Nicaragua and began to prosper in the slave trade.

He still had the desire for adventure. Eventually, he became intrigued by the offer to join Francisco Pizarro's third expedition to Peru. Pizarro first explored the western coast of South America in 1523 and again in 1526. On the second expedition, a raft had been captured bearing silver bracelets, gold crowns, and other riches. These indicated a surprisingly sophisticated civilization somewhere in the region. It would prove to be the remarkable empire of the Inca, which covered some 2,000 miles (3,219 kilometers) along the coast from modern-day Ecuador south to Chile. Pizarro vowed to conquer the Inca.

To Peru

Soto now decided to join Pizarro as a captain in his army. After landing in Peru in 1531, he spent nearly a year with Pizarro's forces traveling through the Andes mountains in South America. Finally, in 1532, they reached the city of Cajamarca, where the Inca ruler Atahualpa lived. Soto was supposedly the first European to make contact with the Inca leader. Most Native American peoples at the time were intimidated by horses, which were not indigenous to the American continents. It is said that Soto rode his horse so close to

Inca ruins at Cuzco, Peru

Atahualpa that the animal's breath ruffled the fringes on the Inca's clothes. But Atahualpa did not move.

Through treachery, of which Soto was a part, the Inca chief was captured and the Inca nation was conquered. From there, Soto went with Pizarro to Cuzco, the capital city of some 200,000 people, which the Spaniards quickly sacked. Part of the reason the Spaniards so easily took control of so many areas in South America was undoubtedly the horse, which gave them a tremendous advantage. Even though the Spanish were generally outnumbered, they were undoubtedly the toughest fighting force in all of Europe, hardened by years of warfare. They also had all kinds of spears and armor to defend themselves, and a tradition of stubbornness that would not let them surrender.

Soto stayed in Peru for nearly three years. However, after Pizarro, as governor, had the Inca ruler executed, Soto grew dissatisfied with Pizarro as a leader. So, Soto returned to Spain in 1536 where he was hailed as a hero for his bravery and bold leadership.

Exploring southern North America

Hernando de Soto had been rich before, but now he was one of the wealthiest of all the returning conquistadors. His part of the Inca campaign alone was 180 pounds of gold and 360 pounds of silver. That was surely enough to settle down to a lavish and gentlemanly lifestyle in Seville. And it was certainly enough to provide a comfortable life for his new bride, Isabel de Bobadilla, daughter of his late patron.

Despite his new lifestyle, Soto was still an adventurer at heart. The romance of the unknown was a greater thrill than any other. A restless Soto used his wealth and reputation to gain an audience with the king, now Charles I of Spain (Charles V of the Holy Roman Empire). He asked for the right to conquer Ecuador and explore the Amazon River basin. Instead, he was appointed governor of Cuba and *adelentado*, or royal deputy, of Florida, which was still unconquered territory. He was ordered to "conquer, pacify, and populate" the region.

About the time Soto was preparing for his journey, Cabeza de Vaca returned to Spain after his long absence with the failed Narvaez expedition. Even though the tales that the survivor told were depressing, they encouraged Soto to think that vast riches could be found in this largely unexplored land. How little explored the region really was can be seen in the maps of the time. On some maps, drawn by Spanish, French, or English cartographers, North America was pictured as a separate continent, but on others it was hooked to Asia. Some maps showed the narrow **isthmus** that separates the Atlantic and Pacific oceans as being about where the North Carolina coastline is now.

Back to America

On April 7, 1538, Soto sailed from Spain in command of 10 ships, 700 men, and 200 horses. His wife Isabel was aboard as well. After arriving in Cuba, Soto almost immediately set about planning the expedition to Florida. When it was ready, he left Isabel as acting governor and sailed to Tampa Bay on Florida's west coast.

Tampa Bay is Florida's largest deepwater port.

Soto landed at Tampa Bay on May 27, 1539, and was immediately attacked by hostile Native Americans. This was the **legacy** left by Ponce de Leon and Narvaez. Soto would do little to dispel the idea among Native Americans that the newcomers were their enemy.

Not long after landing, the expedition was heartened by the discovery of a lost survivor of the Narvaez expedition. Juan Ortiz had been living with Native Americans for about 10 years. He had been on one of the ships that patrolled the coast looking for Narvaez and his men, and was among several of the crew captured by Native Americans. Now fluent in local speech, he became an interpreter for Soto. This was extremely important, since each local tribe often spoke a different language. With Ortiz's help, as the Spaniards entered each new Florida territory, they tried to seek out a Native American who could interpret for them.

Soto planned to head northward in search of gold. Ortiz tried to tell him that no gold existed in the area, but Soto would not listen. He knew of the

An Indian princess offers Soto a pearl necklace.

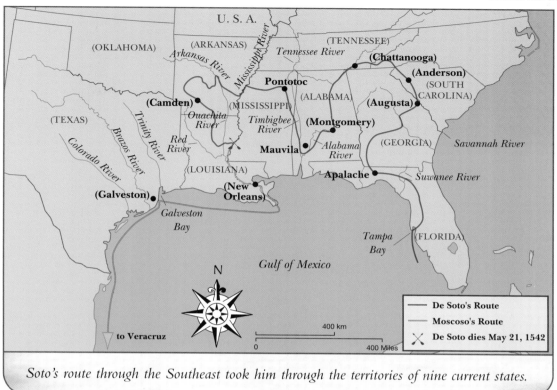

U.S.A.

(OKLAHOMA)   (ARKANSAS)   (TENNESSEE)

Arkansas River   Mississippi River   Tennessee River   **(Chattanooga)**

Pontotoc   **(Anderson)**   (SOUTH CAROLINA)

(Camden)   (MISSISSIPPI)   (ALABAMA)   **(Augusta)**

(TEXAS)   Ouachita River   Timbigbee River   **(Montgomery)**

Trinity River   Red River   (GEORGIA)   Savannah River

Colorado River   Brazos River   **Mauvila**   Alabama River

(LOUISIANA)   **Apalache**   Suwanee River

(Galveston)   **(New Orleans)**

Galveston Bay   Tampa Bay   (FLORIDA)

N

Gulf of Mexico

to Veracruz   400 km   0   400 Miles

— De Soto's Route
— Moscoso's Route
X De Soto dies May 21, 1542

Soto's route through the Southeast took him through the territories of nine current states.

great wealth of the Inca Empire and he believed the tales that spoke of similar treasures in the northern continent.

As Narvaez had done, Soto faced the treacherous swamps of central Florida, dwindling food supplies, and the threat of attack. When they came upon a small Native American village, they often captured the chief and held him for **ransom** until they were given food and guides to the next stop. In this manner, the Spanish reached the village of Apalache, near Tallahassee, where they spent the winter.

Soto left Apalache in the spring of 1540. He headed northward through present-day Georgia. The expedition would eventually explore the Carolinas and Tennessee. But the result was always the same. The gold and riches they sought did not appear. At one point they heard the story of great wealth in pearls to be found at Cofitachequi in present-day South Carolina. The village was said to be ruled by a wealthy and powerful queen.

They arrived in the village, about 75 miles (121 kilometers) from the mouth of the Savannah River, in late April. They met the queen and there were pearls, however, most of the gems were useless. The Native Americans saw no value in the pearls and regularly pierced them to use as ornamental beads. Some of Soto's

An oil painting shows Soto discovering the Mississippi River.

crew wanted to establish a colony there to harvest the pearl supply, but he insisting on moving ahead. They did, however, leave with a supply of some of the precious pearls.

Battle at Mauvila

Soto left the village of the pearls in mid-May 1540 and crossed the Appalachian Mountains, heading for a place called Chiaha, also reported to be rich in gold. Chiaha turned out to be an island (now Burns Island) in the middle of the Tennessee River. There was no gold.

Growing weary and discouraged, Soto and his men headed south again.

At Mauvila (near present-day Choctaw Bluff, Alabama), news reached them that the ships were waiting for them in the Gulf of Mexico. But before they could move on, disaster struck. The Spanish were totally surprised by an attack from a confederation of Native Americans. Although Soto and his men were victorious, routing nearly all of the attackers, their own party was severely crippled, not only losing the pearls but all of its equipment—medical supplies, tools, extra weapons, and bedding.

After resting for a month, Soto made a decision to head north once again, still in search of the elusive treasure. It would prove to be a disastrous choice. Moving through Alabama and then west through Mississippi, the party was constantly attacked by Native Americans. Finally, they set up winter camp about 100 miles (161 kilometers) east of the Mississippi River near present-day Pontotoc, Mississippi. Only Soto's forceful leadership kept the group together.

The big river

Soto left the winter camp in April, after a severe attack by members of the Chickasaw people, which killed eleven Spaniards. The attack may have resulted from Soto's treatment of the Chickasaw during the winter. His methods of dealing with native peoples were extremely harsh. The slightest infraction could result in brutal retaliation or death. For example, if a Chickasaw was found stealing from the Spaniards, his hands were cut off.

On May 21, 1541, Soto and his men became the first Europeans to see the great river of North America, the Mississippi. They named it Rio del Espiritu Santo, which means "river of the Holy Spirit." The site was below what is now Memphis, Tennessee.

The men managed to build barges and cross the river, making their way through Arkansas and Louisiana. Incredibly, Soto was still pursuing reports of gold and silver, this time in the Ozark Mountains. After several fruitless months of traveling, he made winter camp at Camden, Arkansas.

Soto broke camp in March 1542 and headed back toward the big river. At last, he gave up hope of finding great wealth and decided it was time to reach the gulf and the ships. But where was the gulf? Soto sent out scouts to find the way. When they returned saying that the terrain was impossible to travel through, even Soto was discouraged.

He decided they would have to build boats and sail the river to the sea. But on the night of May 21, 1542, worn out from the fruitless search for gold and from the hardships he had endured, Hernando de Soto died of a fever. His men tried to conceal his death, fearing that the Native Americans, who both feared and hated Soto, would find them defenseless without their leader. At first they buried his body in the **compound.** Later, they weighted it with sand and sank it in the waters of the Mississippi.

The last of the Florida expeditions

Knowing he was near death, Soto had appointed Luis de Moscoso de Alvarado to take over command of the severely depleted expedition. Moscoso, who had been with Soto in Peru, ordered the Spaniards to build seven boats. They set sail on the great river on July 2, 1543. Under constant danger from attack, they reached the Gulf of Mexico in 17 days. Then they sailed along the gulf shore and landed in Mexico, near Panuco in the northeast, on September 10. They reached Veracruz in October. Of the original 600 men who started the expedition, 311 survived. In all the territory they explored, except for a few lost pearls, they had found no treasure.

But the expedition did produce one valuable item—a map drawn by Alonso de Santa Cruz. It was not found until his death in 1572. At the time, it quite accurately represented what Europeans knew about the northern gulf coast in the mid-1500s.

The last of the expeditions related to Soto's journey took place in 1549, six years after Moscoco returned to Veracruz. It was led by a Dominican priest, Fray Luis Cancer de Barbastro. He was a Spaniard who had founded a monastery in Puerto Rico in the 1530s. On a trip to Spain in 1547, he presented his plan for a missionary expedition into Florida and was granted a royal order. The priest intended to convert the Native Americans to Christianity through kindness instead of by military force.

In the summer of 1548, Fray Luis returned to Veracruz. Early the following year, along with three priests, Gregorio de Beteta, Juan Garcia, and Diego de Tolosa, and several crew members, the one-ship expedition sailed for Havana. They headed toward Florida after enlisting the aid of a Native American interpreter.

Native Americans were treated harshly by Soto and his men.

Almost immediately after landing at Tampa Bay on May 29, two of the crew and the interpreter were taken prisoner by unfriendly Native Americans Fray Gregorio wanted to turn around and head back, but Fray Luis wanted to rescue the prisoners. They sailed to Charlotte Harbor and sought information at a Native American village. In June Fray Luis saw the captured interpreter, but he failed to rescue her. He did, however, rescue a crew member, Juan Munoz, who had been with Soto years earlier. Munoz told the priest that the Native Americans had killed the other prisoners.

Once again, Fray Gregorio pushed for a return home, but Fray Luis was determined to complete his mission. On June 25, the ship landed on the Florida coast once more. Fray Luis went ashore and was killed by a blow to the head by the Native Americans who greeted him.

The aftermath

Fray Gregorio and the others returned to Mexico with horrific tales of the disaster in Florida. Few understood that Native Americans were no longer willing to be victims of the exploration age. Some records say that Soto's expedition alone killed about 4,000 Native Americans.

Hernando de Soto's journey and those that followed did not find treasure, but they opened much of the southeastern United States to other explorers. Strangely enough, Soto's expedition demonstrates the failure of Spain to establish colonies in North America during the first half of the 1500s. One of the reasons was the land itself, far larger and more rugged than had been imagined back home. The extremes of climate were a shock and often left the expeditions unprepared.

Another reason was the growing resistance of Native Americans. Increasingly, they fought any plans for foreign settlement. Where initially the native peoples had often proved friendly and helpful to the newcomers, they had become wary and then downright hostile when a ship appeared on their shores. A third reason was the wealth that the Spaniards did not find in North America. Convinced that vast riches were hidden somewhere in this land, they often gave up practical attempts to colonize in a frantic search for gold and silver.

Perhaps the biggest reason was the conquistadors themselves. They were soldiers, not statesmen. They sought glory, adventure, and probably most of all gold. They really had no great interest in planting colonies and building civilizations. Not all conquistadors were as cruel as Soto, perhaps, but in general they had no training or disposition to treat native peoples with kindness and respect. It was simply easier to kill or enslave and move on to the next treasure-hunting ground.

Hernando de Soto was probably the perfect example of the professional Spanish soldier in the mid-1500s. He demanded loyalty and obedience, no less than what he himself gave to the church and to the crown. Although he was often cruel and stubborn, his men followed his example through his willingness to share all hardships and dangers alongside them. He is regarded as one of Spain's most able conquistadors and was a great hero of his day.

Chapter Four

Pedro Menendez de Aviles:
Founder of St. Augustine (1565)

I t is the oldest continuously settled city in the United States and boasts the nation's narrowest street. Treasury Street is only seven feet (two meters) wide. About 38 miles (61 kilometers) southeast of Jacksonville, Florida, the city lies at the southern entry of the Atlantic Intracoastal Waterway. Except for the time when Florida belonged to Great Britain (1763–1783), it was the most northern outpost of the Spanish colonial empire for 256 years. It is named for the bishop of Hippo in Algeria, Africa, who lived in the fifth century B.C.E. St. Augustine, Florida, has been part of the United States since 1821.

The founder of this important piece of history was a Spanish explorer who ran away to sea at the age of fourteen. He is often cited as the classic example of the conquistador—loyal, energetic, fearless, and cruel.

A man of the sea

Pedro Menendez de Aviles (1519–1574) was born on February 15 in the seaport of Aviles in Asturias, Spain. His family was land-owning gentry. However, he had so many brothers and sisters—some reports say 20—that the chances of inheriting a fortune were slim. So, like many young European men in those times, he looked to the sea. Indeed, he became one of the most renowned seamen of his day.

A portrait of Pedro Menendez de Aviles (1519–1574)

In 1549, at the age of 30, Menendez was commissioned by Emperor Charles V to drive pirates from the Spanish coast. Later that year while patrolling the shores, he ran into Jean Alphonse, the most feared of all the raiders. Menendez not only boarded the pirate's vessel but fought a duel with him, mortally wounding Alphonse. This and other daring encounters marked Menendez as a seaman of excellent skills and and won him fame and fortune.

He also got a promotion. In 1554, Menendez was named captain of the Indies fleet. This position allowed the holder to amass great personal wealth, often by unethical methods. There is no record that Menendez did so, but by nature he was an impatient man. His concerns were with action, not the endless administrative details of his post. This scant attention to what he regarded as mere details earned him many enemies. They succeeded in getting him imprisoned in 1563. He was released two years later, having regained favor with the Spanish king, Philip II, who took the throne in 1556.

The mission

The king was growing increasingly troubled by reports that a group of French Huguenots had settled on the Florida coast near the mouth of the St. John's River (then the River of May), just north of present-day Jacksonville. Huguenots were Protestants who often suffered severe persecution because of their faith. Philip feared that this settlement would pose a threat to Spanish possessions in Florida.

The Huguenot colony, which included about 70 people with not a farmer among them, was led by Rene de Goulaine de Laudonniere, a mariner and geographer. The Huguenots reached the St. John's River on June 24, 1564. This was the second attempt to establish a French foothold in North America. They had attempted a landing in the same area two years ago. After some indecision, including sailing north and then returning to the original site, they established a colony on June 29 and named it Fort Caroline. It nearly disappeared immediately, almost suffering the same fate as the earlier French colonies. Hunger was a big factor. The French seemed to have no awareness of the fact that these new colonists would need to grow food to eat. It was not long before even the friendly local Native Americans grew tired of the neverending requests for food. Laudonniere quickly sent two ships back to France for supplies and more settlers. But desertion was a problem in the colony and so was the threat of mutiny. They were easy prey for the Spanish.

Meanwhile, the Spanish king had chosen Menendez to lead a colonizing expedition and to deal with the French at Fort Caroline. In addition, Menendez was instructed to build forts along the Florida coastline. They would serve as refuge from pirates and a haven from rough seas for the Spanish fleet returning home loaded with treasure. Menendez sailed in July 1565 with 8 ships and about 1,500 men. Trouble began quickly. One of the ships started to leak and had to turn back. Two went down in a storm off Puerto Rico. So, the fleet that left for Florida from San Juan on August 15 had only about 600 men and five ships.

Land was sighted on August 28, the feast day of St. Augustine. Strangely enough, on that very day, seven French ships, led by Jean Ribault, and more than 600 people had arrived to replenish Fort Caroline! Ribault had commanded the earlier French attempts to colonize.

Menendez entered the bay and formally took possession of Florida and St. Augustine on September 8, 1565, naming it for the saint. Then he established a settlement and fort.

Although he was busy colonizing the area as ordered, Menendez did not forget the other part of his instructions.

This engraving shows Menendez laying out St. Augustine in 1565.

Almost immediately he planned an attack. The French, however, were not unaware of his intentions. They had known for some time that the Spanish resented their presence in the area. Ribault had a plan. Stripping the fort of almost every able-bodied man, the French sailed down to St. Augustine and caught the Spanish by surprise as they were unloading the ships. What could have been disaster for Spain, however, turned into good fortune. A hurricane was approaching and the French ships could not enter the harbor for the attack. In fact, the ships were driven to the south.

Quickly sizing up the situation, Menendez ordered his men to march to the north. It took four days with the hurricane still buffeting the area. They arrived on the morning of September 20 to find Fort Caroline woefully unguarded. Some reports say that Menendez slaughtered the entire Huguenot colony even though he had promised mercy to those who surrendered. The justification for this cruel act was that they were of the "wicked Lutheran sect." Others say he spared the lives of some under the age of fifteen. Whatever the truth, hundreds died. Menendez had their bodies tied to trees with the inscription "Not as Frenchmen but as heretics." Such was the price of being Protestant in the overwhelmingly Catholic lands of the 1500s. Fort Caroline was renamed San Mateo.

Menendez was not finished, however. He sailed south of St. Augustine until he found the inlet where the French ships had sailed and killed all the survivors after they had surrendered, including Ribault. The French had called the inlet the River of Dolphins. Today it is the Matanzas inlet. Matanza means "slaughter" in Spanish.

The French got revenge in 1568 when they destroyed San Mateo. But Spain took it back soon after and kept it through the colonial period.

After the mission

After the massacre of the Huguenots, Menendez carried out his third task. He explored the Atlantic coast and built a series of small forts. The most northern was on St. Helena off present-day South Carolina. Menendez believed that protecting the coast was vital to Spanish control of its empire in America.

No one had any idea of the true size of the North American continent, so Menendez thought that Florida was closer to Mexico than it is. Therefore, he envisioned a roadway through the wilderness. In fact, on two occasions he sent Juan Pardo to explore the region. Both attempts were unsuccessful, with Pardo probably probing no farther west than what is now northern Alabama.

How did they talk?

One of the reasons that many exploration parties in southeastern America were unsuccessful was simply due to a lack of communication between Euro-

Menendez colonizes St. Augustine.

peans and Native Americans. Explorers faced the difficult problem of talking with Native Americans, friendly or not. This was complicated by the fact that native North Americans spoke as many as 24 major languages. Had they all been better able to communicate, the fate of many an expedition and many an explorer might have been far different. In general, the Spaniards had only themselves to blame for a lack of conversation between the two groups. The conquistadors' first response on arriving in the Americas was usually to regard the native peoples as potential

Menendez and his men attack a group of French Huguenots.

slaves, a practice that naturally discouraged free talk on both sides. However, it was not long before explorers began to realize the importance of the Native Americans as guides in this unknown territory. Menendez himself thought of capturing young Native Americans and teaching them Spanish.

Sign language became essential, and drawings or maps were used to communicate. Sometimes the Spaniards tried to get what they wanted by setting a good example. Menendez once ordered some of his soldiers to set up a village near a Native American site in southern Florida. The men were told to "worship regularly," thereby, it was hoped, encouraging friendly relations between the two groups. In this case, the purpose was to get information about the territory, not to convert the people.

On occasion, the explorers were able to take with them Native Americans who had spent some time in Europe.

Even better were the few times when they came upon a sailor who had been shipwrecked or otherwise left behind and had spent years living with native peoples, thus learning the language.

Service in Cuba and the Armada

Menendez was recalled to Spain in 1567, but returned the following year as governor of Cuba. There he established a convoy escort fleet, which helped to protect Spanish treasure ships from being raided by pirates.

By the time of Menendez's governorship, Spain was growing discouraged about settlement in Cuba. Located at the entrance to the Gulf of Mexico, the island—actually made of about 1,600 islands and inlets—was considered a strategic point and a possible source of gold. But few gold supplies were found

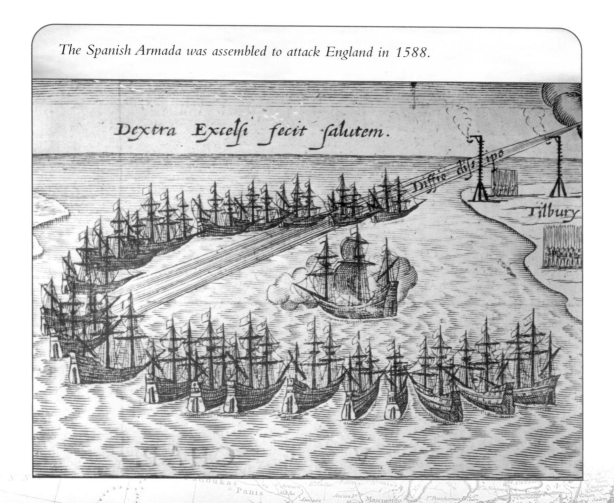

The Spanish Armada was assembled to attack England in 1588.

and this hampered settlement. Instead, the island became more of a staging ground for Spanish explorations along the Gulf coast.

There were probably only a few hundred Spaniards in Cuba when Menendez was governor and fewer than 5,000 Native Americans. The number had drastically declined since the Spanish invasions due to maltreatment and European-brought diseases. The native population was not helped by the fact that Spanish settlers used them as *encomienda*. That was a system giving the conquistadors a certain number of Native Cubans from whom they could exact **tribute** in whatever form. As the Native American population declined, so did the encomienda system.

Menendez left Cuba when Philip II sent for him again in 1572. He was made captain general of the armada being assembled to attack Great Britain. The Spanish Armada was often referred to as the Invincible Armada. It was a great fleet with which Spain intended to defeat the English in 1588. Spain faced the English with an armada of about 130 ships, 8,000 seamen, and about 19,000 soldiers. But the armada that was supposedly invincible was defeated with a loss of about half of its ships. England was saved from invasion.

Menendez never actually commanded the armada, so he did not see his nation's disaster. He died in Spain on September 17, 1574, at the age of 55. His single voyage to the North American mainland left him a lasting tribute in the town of St. Augustine.

St. Augustine today

St. Augustine and its colorful history are good reasons for the flocks of tourists who visit each year. Many of the buildings and sites from Spanish colonial times have been restored, such as San Augustin Antiguo, a recreation of the old Spanish city. The most impressive reminder of Spanish power is the grim, massive Castillo de San Marcos. It is the oldest fort still standing in the United States. The English sea raider Sir Francis Drake took aim on St. Augustine in later years and so did the British general and leader of the Georgia colony, James Oglethorpe. British loyalists used it as a haven during the American Revolution, and Seminoles were imprisoned there during the Indian wars. Union troops moved in during the last three years of the Civil War.

In 1994, a 60-year search ended when archeologist uncovered what they called the "Spanish Plymouth Rock." It was the first fort built by the Spaniards when St. Augustine was founded. The digging had been going on since the 1930s. Ancient maps and records suggested that the fort was in the heart of the city's waterfront area, on the grounds of a Roman Catholic shrine and nearby tourist park. Finally, some artifacts were uncovered in 1980, but it took seven more years for evidence of the actual fort. A moat, about twelve feet (four meters) wide, was uncovered. Digging stopped for lack of funds until 1993 when a charred wooden post was found. Records said that the fort had

been destroyed by fire. Today, a 280-foot (85-meter) aluminum cross, which is dedicated to founder Pedro Menendez de Aviles, stands on the site.

Castillo de San Marcos still stands in St. Augustine today.

Chapter Five

Daniel Boone:
Explorer American Style (1775–1778)

T his story of exploration jumps from 1565 St. Augustine, Florida, to the Cumberland Gap of the Appalachian Mountains in 1775. Much has changed in 210 years. Hernando de Soto or Menendez de Aviles would simply not recognize the place. St. Augustine is still there, as are influences of Spanish culture throughout southeastern North America. But along the Atlantic coastline, from Massachusetts to Georgia, the land belongs to the thirteen colonies of Great Britain. This will soon change, however, because war has just begun between the colonists and the British. It will end with the Treaty of Paris in 1783 and the birth of the United States of America in 1789.

A militia captain during the American Revolution, Daniel Boone (1734–1821) is best known as a frontiersman who became a legendary hero. But he was an explorer, too, playing a large part in the exploration and settlement of what became the state of Kentucky. Like the Spanish conquistadors before him, he was an adventurer. His courage and daring helped to open the American southeast to settlers.

Life on the Frontier

From all the pictures of him, one might think that Daniel Boone sprang to life wearing a **buckskin** suit and carrying

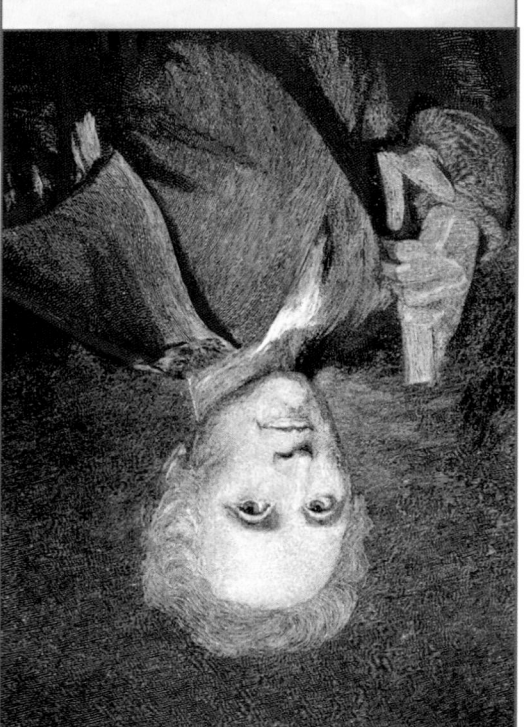

A portrait of Daniel Boone (1734–1821)

a rifle. Such pictures represent a purely American character that had grown since the centuries of early exploration. When Boone was born on November 12, 1734, the area that became the United States had thirteen British colonies and fewer than two million people. Many of them lived where Boone did, in the backcountry. He was

A reconstruction of Daniel Boone's birthplace stands in Berks County, Pennsylvania.

born on a small farm in rural Pennsylvania, about 11 miles (18 kilometers) from present-day Reading.

Colonists in New York and Boston might dress and talk as much as people did in London, but the backcountry folks generally thought of themselves as "American." They were fur traders who learned how to hunt and trap from the Native Americans. Daniel was in fact an expert hunter by the time he was fifteen years old. These "Americans" took over land and worked it with little thought to ownership—a frequent dispute with the native peoples who were there first.

The newcomers tended to have little to do with schooling or too many laws. What they wanted, and frequently fought for, was lots of space and liberty. Out in these wilderness areas, the regulations of the city seemed very far away.

Daniel's parents were Squire and Sarah Morgan Boone, hard-working Quakers. The boy was named for his mother's older brother, who was a traveling Quaker minister. Daniel's grandfather, George, was a farmer who had emigrated from England in 1717. Squire Boone was also a blacksmith and raised cattle, and the boy learned to do everything, including using a rifle, which his father gave him when he was twelve. Boone grew up to be an independent boy who loved the wilderness. Although he had very little formal schooling, he did learn to read and write. That might not seem like much, but in those days Boone's level of education would have been about equal to that of most men in America.

Frontier families such as the Boones tended to be very close knit. They had to face the many hardships and dangers of the wilderness. Their philosophy was to stand together at all costs. The Boones lived on the western edge of European settlement. They often came into contact with Native Americans in the area. In fact, there were many Native American villages within a short distance. Boone grew up in peace with the native peoples and unlike many a frontiersman of the time, never came to hate them. Actually, both white settlers and Native Americans in southeastern Pennsylvania lived much the same way. Their lives centered on hunting. Meat fed families and hides clothed them. Furs could be traded. The men of both groups dressed much alike. They generally wore a fringed hunting shirt sometimes made of deerskin and deerskin moccasins. Beaver hats were in style with the settlers. Both Native American and white men wore their hair long, fixed in braids or knotted, and held in place with bear grease.

Even though the Boones and other **frontier** families often lived in relative peace with Native Americans, things began to change as more and more white settlers began moving west. The settlers began to feel uneasy and Native Americans began to feel resentful. Just as city dwellers today sometimes feel they are being squeezed in by too many people, so did many native peoples. In fact, groups such as the Delaware and Shawnee began pushing west, looking for more space and freedom—and fewer white settlers.

Moving west

About 1749, Squire Boone began to think about moving the family. From his sister and brother-in-law, who had moved to Virginia, he heard that land that was "practically being given away" in the backcountry of North Carolina.

It was an impressive group that left Pennsylvania in the spring of 1750. Three or four Conestoga wagons carried the belongings of Squire and Sarah Boone, their eight unmarried children, including fifteen-year-old Daniel, two married sons and their wives, one married daughter and her husband and baby, plus a nephew and Daniel's best friend, Henry Miller.

The Conestoga wagon was the moving van of the 1700s. It is hard to imagine the West being settled without it. This horse-drawn freight wagon originated in Conestoga Creek, in Lancaster

Conestoga wagons were well-suited to hauling things over difficult terrain.

County, Pennsylvania. Pulled by four to six horses, the wagon could hold up to six tons of supplies and equipment. It often carried the belongings of an entire family. The floor of the wagon curved up on all four sides to keep the contents in place. A white canvas cover was drawn over the wagon to keep out snow and rain.

The Boone family traveled about fifteen miles (24 kilometers) a day, which was about all that was possible due to the weather and the lack of good roads. The travelers spent the winter around Linnville Creek, near what is now Harrisonburg, Virginia. During this period, young Daniel and his friend Henry took hunting forays into the Shenandoah Mountains. One trip indi-cates a trait that would cause Boone some future prob-lems. He just could not seem to hang onto money.

After Boone and Miller had spent some months hunting and trapping while the family was still in camp, the boys took their good-sized bounty of furs and hides to Philadelphia. They were paid a good price for their efforts. But instead of returning home, they spent several days in the city until all their money was spent. Miller later said that it bothered him to end up with nothing after all their hard work. But Boone never seemed to regret it, and in fact, never seemed to be very interest-ed in money at all.

In late 1751, the Boone expedition moved again and finally settled on 640 acres on a fork of the Yadkin River in western North Carolina. The land-scape looked remarkably like what they had left behind.

Boone grew up in this **frontier** land, taking care of the farm with his father. Although he was a hard and steady worker, he took little joy in farming. He was happiest in the fall and winter when he set out to hunt and trap in the woods. This was his life, his occupation, and he became known for miles around as a skilled hunter and trapper.

The Braddock campaign

In 1755, at the age of 21, Boone took part in his first military campaign. The so-called French and Indian War had begun a year earlier. This was the American part of a war between France and Great Britain (1756–1763). The trouble it caused would eventually lead to the American Revolution. The colonists got their first inkling of independence when the British asked them to organize militia against the French in Canada and the West. The British imposed taxes on the colonists to pay for the war against the French, which the colonists felt to be unfair, since they had no representation in the British Parliament.

But, of course, the war was really over which country would eventually win on the North American continent. The British eventually won in 1763, partly because many Native Americans had sided with them. The conflict brought on enormous war debts and great problems in ruling a land from across the sea. Ironically, the victory planted the seeds that would lead to the upcoming American Revolution.

A painting shows General Edward Braddock and his troops near Fort Duquesne during the French and Indian War.

Boone became part of the French and Indian War when he joined the campaign of Major General Edward Braddock, serving as a wagon driver and blacksmith. Braddock had come to North America in 1755 to command all British forces against the French. After several months of preparation, he and his troops set out through the wilderness to attack the French at Fort Duquesne (now Pittsburgh, Pennsylvania). Lieutenant Colonel George Washington of the Virginia militia was one of 700 colonists under his command.

Braddock's force crossed the Monongahela River and marched to a point about eight miles (twelve kilometers) from Fort Duquesne. The commander had only a few scouts for the expedition, even though the chief of the Delawares had offered his services. The British commander had little appreciation for the value of such scouts. As a result, Braddock and his men were ambushed in a ravine by about 254 French and 600 Native Americans. The result was a slaughter on July 9, 1775. Braddock was wounded and carried off the battlefield. He died four days later at Great Meadows, Pennsylvania.

Boone was more fortunate. He was about a half mile back in the line when the ambush started. It went on for some three hours, leaving more than 900 of the original 1,400 men killed or wounded. George Washington had two horses shot from under him but escaped without a wound. Although Boone held his wagon for a while, he finally cut the lead horse free and escaped the carnage.

During the campaign, Boone met hunter John Finley, who told him stories of the magnificent Kentucky wilderness. Finley spoke with excitement about this land west of Virginia on the far slope of the Appalachians. This fired Boone's imagination and he began to think about trekking to Kentucky. First, however, he returned from Braddock's campaign to help his father on the farm once again.

Frontier family life

On August 14 of the following year, he married a neighbor's daughter, Rebecca Bryan. Boone built a log cabin and the couple settled down to farm. Over the next 25 years, they would have 10 children. This was not unusual for the time and place. Most **frontier** couples tended to have many children and, in addition, they would often take in motherless children of relatives. Crowded households were common on the frontier. So was the staggering workload of the women. With the men of the family so often away hunting or trapping, women were left with the entire work of a frontier farm. Without them, the family could not have survived. They cooked and cleaned and washed and sewed, of course. They also wove and spun cloth for clothes. They cultivated the fields and harvested the crops. And unless there were able youngsters around, they fetched water from the spring, chopped

the wood for the fire, and milked the cows. Naturally, if the man of the house-hold happened to be away, the woman would take her rifle outside to find dinner for the family or frighten away intruders.

After the birth of their first child, James, the Boones moved to a small farm on Sugartree Stream, near present-day Farmington, North Carolina. At one point, a raid by Native Americans drove the Boones off their farm and Daniel found work on a tobacco plantation in Virginia. When the Cherokees were defeated in Tennessee, the Boones were able to return to their North Carolina land.

Boone leads settlers through the Cumberland Gap.

About 10 years later, Boone made a trip to Pensacola, Florida, then the capital of the British colony of West Florida. The restless Boone decided that Pensacola was a fine place to settle. His wife, however, didn't like that idea, so Boone went back to farming.

Kentucky on his mind

But Boone was not a farmer at heart. Kentucky was on his mind all this time. In the fall of 1767, with a companion, he set out westward, reaching present-day Floyd County in the east Kentucky mountains. He stayed there until spring. That winter his old friend Finley showed up at the Boone farm, and the two began to plan an expedition into Kentucky. This was the beginning of Boone's fame as an explorer.

On May 1, 1769, Boone, Finley, and four others began their Kentucky venture. With supplies provided by Judge Richard Henderson, who speculated in land, they traveled into northeastern Tennessee and crossed the Cumberland Gap in the Appalachians at the point where Kentucky, Virginia, and Tennessee meet. From there, they traveled north to Station Camp Creek in what is now Estill County in east central Kentucky. Boone became completely enchanted with the Kentucky wilderness.

At the south fork of the Kentucky River, in what is now Daniel Boone National Forest, Boone and a companion were captured by Shawnee raiders. They were held for a week and released unharmed, but without all of their

supplies. After more casualties and a long, hard winter, Boone's brother Squire, who had joined them that winter, went back to North Carolina for more ammunition. Boone would not join him, however, and spent the time alone in the wilderness. By himself, he explored the Ohio River down to near present-day Louisville, Kentucky, as well as the Kentucky and Licking river valleys. When Squire returned with supplies, the two men spent the summer and winter hunting and trapping in the Green and Cumberland River valleys. Finally, it was time to return. Carrying a large supply of furs, they headed back to North Carolina in early 1771. But near the Cumberland Gap, a raiding party of Cherokee appeared. Boone and his brother escaped with their lives, but not with their horses or their furs. So Boone returned home after a two-year absence with nothing to show for it but his enthusiasm for what he called "Kentuck."

Boone the explorer

A restless Daniel Boone was back in North Carolina but in body only. He had lost his heart and his mind to the Kentucky wilderness. He must have been ardent in persuasion. In 1773, a group of 40 settlers plus Boone's own family headed back over the mountains. This time tragedy struck in the Cumberland Gap. They were attacked

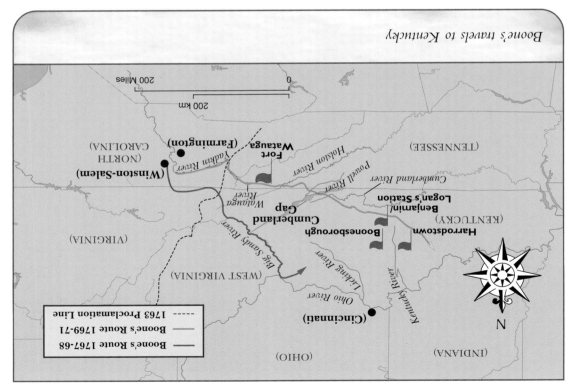

Boone's travels to Kentucky

(OHIO)

(INDIANA)

(TENNESSEE)

(KENTUCKY)

(VIRGINIA)

(WEST VIRGINIA)

(NORTH CAROLINA)

Winston-Salem

Fort Watauga (Farmington)

Cumberland Gap

Boonesborough

Harrodstown

Benjamin Logan's Station

(Cincinnati)

Yadkin River

Watauga River

Holston River

Powell River

Cumberland River

Big Sandy River

Ohio River

Licking River

Kentucky River

N

Boone's Route 1767-68
Boone's Route 1769-71
1763 Proclamation Line

200 Miles
200 km
0

by Native Americans, and Boone's sixteen-year-old son James was tortured and murdered along with five others. Still, Boone refused to give in. When the rest of the party returned to North Carolina, Boone and his family stayed on through the winter in an abandoned cabin before hunger and fear of trouble with the Native Americans forced them to return as well.

When it seemed that Boone's passion would never be realized, his old friend Judge Henderson had a proposition. Having decided that Kentucky was the perfect place to settle, he formed the Transylvania Company to buy land from

The Wilderness Road runs through the Cumberland Gap.

the Cherokee living there. He thought that in time Kentucky would be established as the fourteenth British colony. He hired Boone to be the negotiator of a treaty between the company and the Cherokee for the land.

In March 1775, Boone and 28 men were sent to mark a trail through the Cumberland Gap across Cherokee land as far as the south bank of the Kentucky River. Thus the Wilderness Road was built. Some 300 miles (483 kilometers) long, it ran from eastern Virginia to the interior of Kentucky, ending at the Ohio River at Louisville. Officially named the Wilderness Road in 1796, when it was widened to allow the passage of Conestoga wagons, it soon became the main route of travel into what Americans referred to simply as "the West." The road helped make possible the first settlements in Kentucky. By the time Kentucky became a state in 1792, about 70,000 settlers had been lured over the Cumberland Gap to the Wilderness Road and beyond. By the 1820s, it would become the main southern highway to the West.

Building the Wilderness Road was a tremendous task. The men had to join bison trails with woodland paths, hack down forests, roll away boulders, and avoid Native Americans. Guide markers had to be posted at difficult sites.

Boone lost no time in hacking out a trail in the wilderness and in establishing his long-dreamed-of settlement. In April 1775 he began building a fort on the Kentucky River. It became Boonesboro, the first settlement in Kentucky along with Harrod's Town and Benjamin Logan's. Later that year, Boone's wife and daughter joined him in Boonesboro. Today Boonesboro is a resort village within Daniel Boone State Park.

The war years and beyond

Although the first Kentucky settlements prospered, Henderson's idea for the fourteenth colony did not. Instead, it was annexed to Virginia as a county. Boone was appointed a captain in the county militia during the American Revolution. He spent his time defending the Kentucky settlements from Native American attacks and in guiding parties of new settlers to the territory.

In 1778, Boone was captured by the Shawnee and adopted as a son of the chief, Blackfish. At first he was taken to Detroit, which was a British outpost, and then moved to a camp in Chillicothe, Ohio. After five months, Boone escaped in June and made his way back to Boonesboro where he warned the settlement of an impending British and Indian attack. When it came in September, the settlement successfully weathered a ten-day siege.

Upon his return to Boonesboro, Boone discovered that his wife had given him up for dead and returned to North Carolina. He went back to get her and returned to Kentucky in October with a new group of settlers in 1779.

A photograph of Boone's home in Femme Osage, Missouri.

But now there was trouble with the settlers' claims to land in Kentucky. Since Henderson's idea for a separate colony had been refused, the land deeds that he had issued to the new settlers were not valid. So, the settlers scraped together $20,000 to legally purchase their land. They gave the money to Boone to take to the Virginia capital of Richmond. Not far from Boonesboro, he was robbed of the entire amount. Perhaps it was just because he moved around so much, but Boone certainly seems to have been a magnet for robbers on the **frontier**.

Boone returned emptyhanded and moved his home west. In 1780, Kentucky was divided into three counties. Boone

was made lieutenant-colonel of Fayette County, and the following year was elected to the Virginia legislature. Since the American Revolution was still being fought, the legislature was forced to meet in Charlottesville.

Not long afterward, a British raiding party surprised the town, capturing Boone and several others. However, they were held for only a few days and then released.

But Boone returned home to more trouble, now from Native Americans. His farm was attacked, killing his brother Edward. In another attack near Lexington, his son Israel was killed. Such problems led to a major campaign in the area to drive native peoples away from the colonists' settlements. It was led by George Rogers Clark, a frontier military leader who spent the war years in Kentucky and along the Ohio River. He drove the Shawnee from Chillicothe and Piqua and destroyed Shawnee villages in the Miami, Ohio, River valley. After the Revolution, he was appointed Indian commissioner by the new U.S. government and helped to negotiate a treaty with the Shawnee.

Moving on

Daniel Boone may have been a brave fighter and daring explorer, but he surely was no businessman. He apparently gave away a good deal of land to his children, was cheated out of it by others, and improperly registered land claims for the rest. The first of many eviction suits began in 1785. Eventually, Boone lost all the land he had ever settled.

In 1786, the Boones moved to Mayville on the Ohio River above Cincinnati. They opened a tavern and a store for river travelers. But Boone never seemed able to stay long in one place, so in two years they abandoned his beloved Kentucky to move to Point Pleasant at the mouth of the Kanawha River in what is now West Virginia.

The Boones opened another store, which Rebecca operated while Boone himself hunted and trapped. In 1791, with the Revolution over and the U.S. Constitution adopted, Boone was chosen to represent his county in the Virginia legislature. The Boones stayed in Kanawha County (which eventually became part of West Virginia) for a few years, but in 1799 they were on the move once again.

Boone's son, Daniel Morgan Boone, had moved to the Spanish territory of Louisiana (now Missouri) in 1796, where he founded the settlement of Femme Osage on the Missouri River near the town of St. Charles. The Boones moved there in 1799, and stayed there for eleven years. Boone continued to hunt and trap, but he also served in the Spanish administration until the territory was turned over to the French. It later became part of the United States under the Louisiana Purchase of 1804.

Perhaps he would have moved anyway, but Boone was always bothered by the debts he had incurred through his poor handling of claims back in Kentucky. So, he and Rebecca returned in 1810. Boone did manage to pay off his debts, although it left him penniless once again. In fact, according to the often-told story, he was debt-free with 50 cents in his pocket.

After Rebecca died in 1813, Boone lived with his son Nathan until his death in 1820. He was 85 years old. It is said that he was so frail that he could barely walk around the cabin. The only portrait of him painted from life was done in 1820, three months before he died. Young painter Chester Harding traveled to the tiny trading town of St. Charles. At first, Boone refused to sit for a portrait, but he finally agreed, although a friend some-times had to steady his head while Harding was painting.

Although Boone was physically weak, Harding saw that his eyes were still stern and he had not lost his wit. When the painter mentioned reading that the great trapper Boone himself was once lost in the woods for three days, Boone would admit only that, "I was bewildered once for three days."

Harding may have read of Boone's adventures in the first book that brought his name to the general public. It was by John Filson, entitled "The Discovery, Settlement and Present State of Kentucke ... To which is added An Appendix.

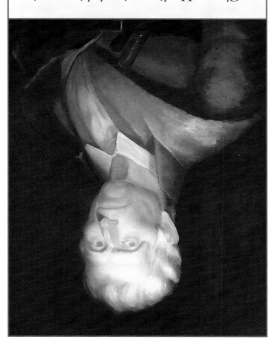

Chester Harding painted this portrait of Boone as an older man.

Containing The Adventures of Col. Daniel Boon." It was published on Boone's 50th birthday in 1784.

When the book was read abroad, he achieved international fame as well. However, the critics thought it immature, romanticized, full of errors, and not at all a true picture of the **frontier** man. Reportedly, Boone claimed that there was not a lie in it!

The legacy

Daniel Boone was a hero when he died, and through the years, he grew into one of the nation's most respected and

A painting shows hunter, trapper, and explorer Daniel Boone in his familiar buckskin clothes and coonskin cap.

admired figures. With his **buckskin** shirt, **coonskin** cap, and hunting rifle, he has be-come a larger-than-life figure, a romantic vision of the old frontier. Surely, Daniel Boone could not have been as tall or as brave or as strong or as honest as the stories paint him to be.

Actually, Daniel Boone was not a tall man, about five feet eight inches (1.7 meters). He was powerfully built, with short arms and thick legs. He had blue-gray eyes and dark hair, which he wore Indian-style. Although he was not educated, he apparently had a great deal of natural intelligence, except perhaps when it came to land claim matters. He was by all records a truthful, honest, and quiet man. He seemed to be at peace with himself, able to spend days and months alone in the wilderness. He was never known to become unduly excited by events, which perhaps is why he harbored no particular ill will toward Native Americans even though they brought him great sorrow over the years.

Numerous books have been written about Daniel Boone. In 1833, Timothy Flint, Boone's first biographer, published *Biographical Memoir of Daniel Boone, the First Settler of Kentucky.* It went to 14 editions and became a best-seller of the time.

Although Flint captured the frontiersman as a hero with a passion for wandering, Boone was not really larger than life. Unlike the conquistadors, he did not have their power, and probably not the desire, to accomplish deeds by force. He was not the discoverer of Kentucky, as some called him, or even its first white settler or explorer. He might better be called the first white Westerner. For "where the West began" depended on when the question was asked. In the 1600s, the West would have been just past the Atlantic coastline.

By the time of the American Revolution, it had about reached the crest of the Appalachian Mountains. It was Daniel Boone who forged the highway from there into the unknown territory.

Boone is an important part of American history. He had the qualities needed by the American explorer of **frontier** days—courage, strength, leadership, and determination. Being an excellent hunter and trapper did not hurt either. And by using those qualities as well as he knew how, Daniel Boone did a great service to his country. Without Boone, Kentucky's history might be far different. He helped to open the lands of southeastern North America, which in turn opened the great floodway to the American West.

What Did They Find?

Exploration is an overlapping kind of work. One explorer learns from the previous one about what to do or what not to do. This is not always successful, but it is better than starting out with no knowledge at all. When Ponce de Leon made his first voyage to the Americas in 1493, Christopher Columbus was on his second trip. When Ponce de Leon sailed to Florida, his explorations took away some of the mystery of this strange new land. That made nations—and certainly explorers themselves—more willing to travel into unknown territory. Hernando de Soto went even farther, all the way to the Mississippi River.

These explorers in southeastern North America began the long process of change on the continent. The explorations of Narvaez and de Vaca, although not as well known as most, brought new information to the Spanish. While centuries have passed since Menendez founded the city of St. Augustine, the southeastern United States still has a strong Spanish flavor in its architecture and customs. This is part of the heritage that the Spanish explorers left in North America.

When Daniel Boone helped to build the Wilderness Road and explore what would be the state of Kentucky, the thirteen British colonies were becoming a nation. Like explorers before him, he helped to open the land to newcomers.

The deeds of these explorers of southeastern North America read like an exciting adventure novel, because adventure is what they were all about. The conquistadors were daring men, brave and often foolhardy. Some were well educated for their time; many were considered cruel even in an age when cruelty was little noticed. Whatever their shortcomings, they along with the later adventurer Daniel Boone wrote many pages in the history of the North America continent. It is those records and tales of what they did and saw that give us some understanding of what we are today.

Important Events in the Exploration of Southeastern North America

1493	Ponce de Leon sails to the Americas on second voyage of Christopher Columbus; first European to see Puerto Rico
1498	Panfilo de Narvaez emigrates to Hispaniola
1502	Ponce de Leon returns to West Indies from Spain, subdues Higuey tribe in Dominican Republic
1507–08	Ponce de Leon explores Cuba; becomes governor
1509	Narvaez goes to Jamaica
1511	Narvaez in brutal conquest of Cuba; becomes governor
1513	Ponce de Leon becomes first European explorer in Florida
1514	Hernando de Soto sails to Panama
1515	Ponce de Leon returns to Puerto Rico
1520	Narvaez is sent to Mexico to capture Cortes; is defeated and imprisoned; loses an eye in battle
1521	Ponce de Leon settles Caparra (Old San Juan); wounded in battle and dies of wounds in Cuba; Narvaez is released from prison
1523	Soto sent to Nicaragua on mission; settles there
1527	Narvaez sails from Spain to colonize Florida
1528	Narvaez lands near Tampa Bay; claims Florida for Spanish king; explores northern Florida to Tallahassee; sails along Gulf of Mexico coast in October; is lost at sea
1531	Soto joins Pizarro in conquest of Peru
1536	Cabeza de Vaca, survivor of Narvaez failed expedition makes his way to Mexico; Soto returns to Spain
1538	Soto sails to Florida
1539	Soto lands at Tampa Bay

1540	Soto explores northern Florida, Carolinas, Tennessee, and Georgia looking for gold
1541	Soto is first European to see Mississippi River, May 21
1565	Pedro Menendez de Aviles lands at St. Augustine, Florida; claims land for king; slaughters Huguenot colony at Fort Caroline
1568	Aviles is named governor of Cuba
1559	Body of Ponce de Leon reburied in San Juan Cathedral, Puerto Rico; city of Ponce later named for him
1751	Daniel Boone moves to western North Carolina from Pennsylvania
1755	Boone fights in French and Indian War
1767	Boone first explores Kentucky
1768	Boone begins Kentucky exploration for two years
1773	Boone takes settlers into Kentucky; is attacked at Cumberland Gap and son is killed
1774	Boone is sent to mark Wilderness Road through Cumberland Gap; builds Boonesboro
1778	Boone is captured by Shawnee for five months
1786	Boone moves to Mayville and opens store on Ohio River
1791	Boone becomes member of Virginia legislature after the Revolution
1796	Boone moves to Spanish territory of Louisiana (now Missouri)
1810	Boone moves back to Kentucky to pay off debts
1813	Boone moves to St. Charles on the Missouri River
1821	Boone dies in St. Charles

Glossary

buckskin soft, pliable leather worn by American frontiersmen

compound fenced-in area containing a group of buildings

coonskin fur of a raccoon usually made into a hat worn by frontiersmen

doctrine statement of government or religious policy

epidemic sudden spread or growth, as of a disease

flotilla fleet of ships, generally large

frontier region beyond settled or developed country

isthmus narrow land strip connecting two larger land areas

legacy something received from an ancestor or from the past

panhandle narrow projection of a larger territory, such as in Florida

ransom money paid in exchange for someone or something that has been kidnapped or stolen

squire in ancient times, an armor bearer in the service of a knight or nobleman

tribute payment to ruler or nation as a sign of submission or as payment for protection

Further Reading

Cabeza de Vaca, Alvar Nunez, and Harold Augenbraum. *The Chronicle of the Narvaez Expedition*. New York: Viking Penguin, 2002.

Faragher, John Mack. *Daniel Boone: Life and Legend of an American Pioneer*. New York: Henry Holt, 1993.

Fuson, Robert H. *Juan Ponce de Leon and the Spanish Discovery of Puerto Rico and Florida*. Blacksburg, Va.: Mcdonald & Woodward, 2000.

Goetzmann, William H., and Glyndwr Williams, *The Atlas of North American Exploration: From the Norse Voyages to the Race to the Pole*. Norman, Okla.: University of Oklahoma Press, 1998.

Roberts, Russell. *Pedro Menendez de Aviles*. Bear, Del.: Mitchell Lane, 2002.

Saari, Peggy and Daniel B. Baker. *Explorers & Discoverers: From Alexander the Great to Sally Ride*. Detroit: Gale, 1999.

Whitman, Sylvia. *Hernando de Soto and the Explorers of the American South*. New York: Chelsea, 1991.

Index